Stellar Resume Writing: Secrets from a Corporate Recruiter

"This book is great for those that are trying to build their resume and get hired by the right company. I basically built a brand new resume right after I read this book and I got an internship offer from the company I have been wanting to work for. I learned so much from this book. I was always trying to improve my resume and this book gave me a lot of tips that I had never tried before. There is something for everyone in this book."

— Tae Yoo, *KU Engineering Student*

"If you are trying to make a perfect resume, this book is definitely for you. It will save you at least several hours go to career workshops. Everything you need to know about resume is inside the book. The book is concise and focus on the main idea. Last but not least, do you want to get advice from an experienced recruiter or just some random blog writers? I would choose the voice of an experienced recruiter. I highly recommend this book."

— Mai Bui, M.S., *Process Engineer*

"I had the great pleasure of speaking with the author about my own resume and job search. His feedback and suggestions were amazingly on point and greatly aided me in building a solid resume that eventually lead to an interview and job offer an hour afterwards!

Resume writing can be a very daunting undertaking, and few people from the "inside" will tell you what they didn't like about yours. Information like this is invaluable!

Thanks so much!"

– James Henry, *HR Manager*

"If you're serious about building your resume in a way that will attract interest, then you should read this book. It's full of nuggets every job seeker needs.

As a former engineering recruiter myself, I know what recruiters and hiring managers are typically looking for, and that's what Greg gives you here. He's a recruiter too, so he knows what he's talking about. He tells you what he likes...and what frustrates him. His honesty, if applied, will get you more interviews."

– Don Gallagher, *Former Engineering Recruiter*

Stellar Resume Writing

Secrets from a Corporate Recruiter

How to Land Interviews

Also by Gregory Austin

Interviewing for Success *(forthcoming)*

The Art of Networking *(forthcoming)*

Stellar Resume Writing

Secrets from a Corporate Recruiter

How to Land Interviews

by

Gregory Austin

For more related content, visit:

http://www.stellarresumewriting.com

Cover by Brian Gregg

Edited by Patricia Austin and Chris Wynter

ISBN: 9781796859201
Imprint: Independently published

Table of Contents

INTRODUCTION

Thank you for purchasing the book, "Stellar Resume Writing – Secrets from a Corporate Recruiter. How to Land Interviews." I designed this short book to read more like a workbook or a how-to document to give you some tangible and tactical knowledge to pour into your resume and help you get noticed by a desirable employer.

A Little About The Author

I have been a recruiter for over 8 years. I started in agency recruiting during which companies would pay me a fee to find them candidates who would be an excellent fit for their organization.

During that time, I learned how to best present candidates so that they would most likely get an interview. I take pride and enjoyment out of coaching job-seeking clients with their resumes, job search, communications, interviewing prep, and negotiations.

In the past few years, I have been a corporate recruiter who finds quality candidates for the company I work for. In that capacity, I have learned, from the inside, what hiring managers are really looking for and what they really want to see.

I have placed candidates from the front line in customer service or factory positions to accountants, pharmaceutical scientists, sales managers, engineering managers, marketing professionals, IT professionals, directors, and a CFO.

I have direct experience in the following industries: manufacturing, healthcare IT, pharmaceutical, biotechnology, non-profit, conferences/symposia, real estate, law enforcement, academia, telecommunications, consulting, business intelligence, AI, construction, commodities, and retail.

I have traveled to California, Boston, Denver, St. Louis, Portland, North-Central Florida, Savannah, Charlotte, Cincinnati, Philadelphia, New Jersey, Washington DC, Baltimore, Houston, Raleigh-Durham, Atlanta, Providence, Tulsa, Las Vegas, Dubai, and India. I have worked with candidates from the U.S., Canada, Mexico, India, China, Korea, Bangladesh, Nigeria, Egypt, Jordan, Vietnam, Haiti, and others.

I can relate to just about anyone, from anywhere, across a multitude of industries and fields.

Between these experiences and having read thousands of resumes during those years, I have boiled it down to the essential elements you need in your resume to land that interview!

If you are a beginner at writing a resume, getting back into the job market after a long career, or a seasoned resume writer looking for some higher-level tips, you can find value in this book.

While there are some very good best practices that I will cover and some things you absolutely must do, there is no perfect resume for every hiring manager/employer. Some hate resumes over one page, some like long commentaries, while some prefer CV (curricula vitae) style resumes that detail every job you worked since you were 14, etc.

I have scaled it down to the essentials that the vast majority of hiring managers will key in on. There are certain things you must do!

On your resume, you MUST have your contact information easy to read, your education, and your detailed job history (with dates and titles). You MUST also have a format that is easy to read and follow, and you MUST NOT have any spelling errors or incorrect information.

During my recruiting career, I have always found the most pleasure in helping candidates, especially those whom I knew I couldn't hire at that particular time and whom also needed some help to better their game. I'm passionate about helping candidates gain more confidence in their own job search and in giving them more tools to be successful. I want to help YOU get that next job!

Disclaimer: In any of the examples I use in this book, all personally identifiable information (names, companies, contact information, etc.) have been changed to protect anonymity.

Your Resume is Your Personal Brand … and Your Ticket to the Show

Your resume represents who you are and should reflect your personal brand. **What is a personal brand?** It is who you are, what you do, what you stand for, your identity, and how it relates to the world. In the case of a resume, it means how you relate to the business or vocational world (for academic and non-profit entities).

Your brand should represent your "profession", what you really excel at, not just the job you do. For example, let's say you have 10 years' experience as a Civil Engineer in designing bridges. You're not just an engineer who can throw together some structural drawings; you are a Civil Engineering, Bridge-Designing Expert.

Perhaps you're a nurse who has spent most of your career taking care of infants. In that case, you're not just a trained nurse who can work in a hospital, doctor's office, or nursing home; you are a Neonatal Nursing Expert who helps save the lives of new babies.

In any case, your expertise, that area in which you excel in the most, is your personal brand and your resume should reflect that. It should be easy to read and understand exactly what you bring to the table and what "impact" you can make in an organization.

Unfortunately, a lot of people think that because of their position in a company (for example a data entry clerk or warehouse worker), that they couldn't possibly make an impact in a company, let alone a big one, but that's simply not true.

There are many candidates out there, and companies truly need them to make the organization run smoothly, to create products and get them out the door, to take care of their customers, etc. Even if it's something as simple as highlighting your proven record of dependability and reliability, that you show up on time every day and put in a solid effort during each shift. Most companies will genuinely value this, and if shown over time, it will be the springboard for other growth opportunities down the road.

I've seen many employees start at an entry-level position, even with a lesser education, move up and up until they were running a department or even became a Vice President. Your resume doesn't need to detail every little thing you've ever done in your career, but it IS your Ticket to the Show.

The Show being the Interview. You want to whet their appetites enough to get in front of them, then share more details on how you can make a real impact in their company.

Shotgun vs. Targeted Job Search

There are basically two ways to go about a job search. One is what I call the "Shotgun" method, which is what most people default to, especially if they find themselves unexpectedly on the job market or otherwise feel a certain amount of desperation to land that new or next job. Of course, the longer you are out of work, then the more desperate you become.

Alternatively, it could be because you are so miserable in your current job, you are willing to take the first thing that comes along to escape your situation. The **"Shotgun"** method is when you shoot out your resume to as many job openings as quickly as possible.

The **"Targeted"** method is a much more methodical, thought out and time-consuming approach. Each way has its pros and cons.

The Shotgun Method

The Shotgun Method may seem like a good idea, especially in this day and age in which applying to jobs has become faster and easier. Also, you may think, "Why spend time in researching potential companies when I just need a job??" If that's the case, and you need to put food on the table, then this approach may be necessary. But bear in mind that your next job will likely be a <u>short hop</u>, or worse, another blip on your resume that starts to scream "Job Jumper" to potential employers down the road who may very well pass on giving you a call since they believe you won't stick around for them either.

What has made the Shotgun Method easier, and more dangerous, than ever is the advent of mobile apps such as Indeed Mobile and Zip Recruiter. After you upload your resume on Indeed and Zip, you can download the Indeed Mobile and/or Zip Recruiter apps and easily apply to jobs searchable on each app. In most cases, the mobile online applications are set up for an "easy" apply by pressing a button or swiping on your phone. This makes applying for the job very fast and very easy.

While this is a nice reprieve from so many of the extraordinarily long application processes forced upon you by many employers (especially healthcare, government, and university sites), it can be an overly tempting option. You may apply to jobs for which you are not at all qualified for, apply to many positions in the same company, or worse, miss out on an opportunity to customize your resume to a job that is highly desirable. Let me cover the dangers and pitfalls involved in each option.

The Targeted Job Search Method

The Targeted Job Search Method is by far the best approach to take. It does take time and discipline, but it is worth it! In this approach, you "target" companies that fit the criteria most important to you. It could be the industry, company size, company reputation, corporate culture, people you know in the company, etc.

Some candidates only want to work for Fortune 500 companies. While some prefer smaller, privately held companies or only government jobs. Others will just consider companies in the technology sector, or manufacturing, or healthcare. You get the idea.

If you already know what kind of company and role you have been most happy in, then you are better off aiming at those targeted companies to improve the odds of job satisfaction.

You can never be 100% sure about that, so you want to research their company website to gain insights into their culture. Also, websites like Glass Door, Google and Indeed accept reviews of companies, their culture, corporate leadership, benefits and interview process.

Glass Door is the biggest of these review sites, and they have captured a lot of data, but please take it with a grain of salt. Keep in mind most of the people who leave a review are either very happy or very unhappy, even angry at the company.

Many of those disgruntled reviewers got fired for poor performance, poor attendance, poor attitude or a combination of the above. You will find truths and exaggerations in most of the reviews. If you find a company that is over 3.5 stars, it's a great find. If a company is below 2.5 stars, you should probably avoid it. There are likely some serious issues going on there.

Check for high turnover and consistent management problems, especially from the top. Some companies look amazing from the outside and in the general press, but once you look under the hood, you find out they don't treat their people well and fail to provide reasonable work-life balance.

I could go on and on about resume writing and hiring theories, but I know that you are ready to dig in and either get your resume created from scratch or provide that needed tune-up to sharpen your resume. So, let's get started!

CHAPTER 1: ELEMENTS OF A GREAT RESUME

There are 9 elements of a great resume:
1. Form: <u>Chronological</u> over Functional Resumes
2. One-Pager vs. Many-Paged Resumes
3. Basic Formatting
4. Contact Information
5. Professional Skills/Accomplishments
6. Education and Certifications
7. Professional Experience *in Reverse Chronological Order*
8. Awards, Patents or Publications
9. Volunteer Work and Interests

These are the 9 elements that I have learned during my career to have the greatest impact on the most important resume "reader", the hiring manager! The last element "Awards, Patents, or Publications" is optional and only relevant if you have any relevant awards, patents or publications in your professional life.

1. Form: Chronological over Functional Resumes
For some, this may seem like Greek to you. If it is, then you are probably already using a chronological format, and you can skip this section if you like. If you're not familiar with what a functional resume is, then let me define it for you. A "Functional" resume

is one that describes in detail what you have done in your career, usually in paragraph form, then your titles and job history is written at the bottom in one-liners.

Example excerpt from a functional resume:

EXPERIENCE
In my accounting career, I have specialized in cost accounting, general ledger, journal entries, and auditing review. I managed over 20 accountants in my career and have strong experience in Great Plains Dynamics software. I have always met deadlines when closing the books, etc., etc., ...

JOB HISTORY
Controller, Smith Co.	6/2011 - present
Asst. Controller, Johns Co.	4/2005 - 6/2011
Accounting Manager, ABC co.	1/2000 - 4/2005
Staff Accountant, 123 Co.	5/1995 - 1/2000

Although I get to read about your accomplishments in detail and I can clearly see what your job history is, I have NO idea *when* you accomplished them. Furthermore, most recruiters, like myself, and hiring managers are more pressed for time than ever, so reading a long narrative can be annoying and sometimes those resumes <u>don't even get read</u>.

Being able to quickly spot required skill sets and accomplishments in bullets under the job titles, and instantly view what jobs and time periods during which they happened, makes it dramatically easier to sort and spot needed talent and get those preferred candidates on the phone more rapidly.

What I've just described is the pattern of a Chronological Resume format, which is highly preferred. I'm sure there are some hiring managers out there who prefer a Functional Resume format, but I've yet to meet one.

2. One-Pager vs. Many-Paged Resumes

I have seen too many candidates stress far too heavily on this question, "Don't I have to fit it into 1 page? Won't the hiring manager toss it if it's too long?" I can't speak for every hiring manager, but generally speaking, no. Your resume should fit relative to the position you are applying to and to the extent of your work history.

If you have had a long career, then it behooves you to mention your career progression, especially if it is relevant to your career field or demonstrates other experience that applies to the job description.

Overall, I don't advise to leave out much because most recruiters and hiring managers want to understand what you have done and when you did it, to get the full picture of your career progression, warts and all. If you leave out significant job history, only to regurgitate it during the interview, it generally doesn't look good for you at that point.

It's always better to be upfront, even if the story is less than ideal, so it shows your character and integrity. It's better to tell your story when it didn't work out so well and be able to then share what you learned from that experience.

We're all human, but if the story is particularly bad, then it may make sense to omit something from the distant past as long as it doesn't become a gap in your resume you will have to answer for. Then it just appears as if you are trying to cover something up.

Best practices dictate the you should not omit important job history or accomplishments just to make it fit one page. Also, do not use a very small font or extended paragraph format to squeeze it down to one page either. The ease of reading your resume is far more critical.

However, if you feel compelled to use the one-page format, even you have quite a bit of job history, then the format used below is an effective one. I recently came across this resume and was impressed by how he included so much relevant and quality content in an easy to digest, one-page format. He was able to include accomplishments, technical skills, and other achievements. It didn't take him long to land a good position.

John Doe

I have spent the past twenty years developing technical solutions for complex business needs in the financial services industry. I want to apply the skills I've developed to help your organization meet its clients' needs, and I want to help to foster a positive corporate culture.

1234 Main St.
Anytown, MO 66222
(816) 555-1212
johndoe@gmail.com

EXPERIENCE

ABC Systems, Anytown MO — *Senior Software Engineer*
SEPT 1993 - PRESENT

- Substantial development experience with a host of different tools and technologies, such as Java, JQuery, JavaScript, SQL Server, REST and WSDL services, HTML, CSS, XML/XSL and JSON.
- Developed talent at understanding the client's business and collaboratively designing solutions that met their core needs.
- Held a series of technical and managerial positions at DST.
- Experience managing divisions of up to 25 associates, as well as remotely managing international development teams.
- Involved in a program to mentor younger associates.
- Developed a quality control sampling methodology that saved over a half million dollars annually.
- Core team member on the largest client conversion in company history in our legacy mutual fund account tracking system.
- Developed a pioneering thin client customer service application for the cable industry, which led to a fifteen-year relationship with the largest customer in DST's BPS division.
- Trained hundreds of DST and client employees on a custom reporting tool.

EDUCATION

Northwestern University, Evanston IL — *M.S. in Marketing*
AUG 1990 - DEC 1991

- Northwestern University Fellowship recipient
- Financed 100% of tuition and living expenses through fellowship and an entrepreneurial award

University of Iowa, Iowa City IA — *B.B.A. in Marketing and Human Resources Management*
AUG 1987 - MAY 1990

- President's and Dean's Lists
- State of Iowa Math and Science Scholar
- Financed 50% of tuition and expenses through scholarships, full time retail management and sales positions and an internship.

TECHNICAL SKILLS

Substantial development and support experience with Java, JavaScript, JQuery, HTML, SQL, DB2, Oracle, XML/XSL, JSON, CSS, ASP, WSDL, REST, SOAP, COBOL, Visual Basic, IIS, Linux, and JCL. Extensively utilized Microsoft Visual Studio, Eclipse, SQL Developer, Fiddler, Web Application Stress Tool, WireShark, SoapUI, XMLSpy and many other developer tools.

AWARDS AND VOLUNTEERISM

Volunteer of the Year for the Greater Anytown YMCA

Spirit of Service recipient for the Greater Anytown YMCA

President of the Board of Directors for the Anytown YMCA

Board of Directors for the Secret Order of the Key, Inc

Vice President of the church council at Lutheran Church

Member of Mensa

Eagle Scout

HOBBIES

Extensive experience in homebrewing, having produced award-winning beers.

Play guitar in local cover bands

Enjoy bicycling, travel, and cooking.

3. Basic Formatting, Consistency and Detail

This is an area in which many job seekers miss the mark in one way or another. They don't use bullets to make their skills and accomplishments stand out, they use more than one font, they make it hard to follow their job history, have poor use of bolding or underlining, or they just don't proofread and spell-check.

Using sentence fragments and some "looser" grammar is acceptable in most resumes as long as you are making it very clear how your skill sets are going to help the company solve their problems (provided you're not applying for a Writing position that is).

There are so many ways candidates have made it difficult for the reader (their potential new employer) to quickly evaluate their skills and experience to determine if they may be a fit.

There are some basic steps you can take to make your abilities jump off the page and grab their attention. So, be sure to use the SAME font throughout your whole resume and be consistent with your formatting. If you use a 12-point font for the company names in your job history and a 10-point font for the job detail, then keep that same formatting consistent throughout your job history. It makes for a much more appealing and professional looking resume.

Let's observe a couple of examples:
Poor example:

COMPANY1, Hamilton, OH
2015 – 2017
Recruiting Manager
> Responsible for the full lifecycle of recruiting for a local call center and coorporate recruiting roles.
> Hiresd 618 new employees in 2016.
> Lead a team of 3 in the recruiting department
> Effecctive Change Management is addressed as an ongoing need at the Site level.

Responsible for recruiting/sourcing marketing and sourcing strategies across many modalities: job fairs, TV, radio, multiple job boards Facebook Twitter LinkedIn YouTube, Instagram other digital platforms Tools used: iCiMS, Taleo Lawson ADP Excel Word PowerPoint.

COMPANY2, Overland Park, KS April
2013 – **December 2014**
Talent Acquisition Specialist
> Responsible for the full lifecycle of recruiting for the organization both locally and nationally. Successfully placed over 90 associates in Sales, Marketing (creative/tactical), Product Marketing, Accounting/Finance (revenue recognition), Consulting, Project Managers, Operations, IT (security, support, developers), and Healthcare (Accountable Care, Meaningful Use).Interact with all levels of executive leadership to understand hiring plan priorities and job requirementsDirectly responsible for posting, sourcing, screening, managing internal interview process, offer negotiations, and onboarding of experienced professionals

18

Good example:

COMPANY1, Hamilton, OH   January 2015 – June 2017
Recruiting Manager
- Responsible for the full lifecycle of recruiting for a local call center and corporate recruiting roles.
- Hired 618 new employees in 2016.
- Led a team of 3 in the recruiting department
- Effective Change Management is addressed as an ongoing need at the Site level.
- Responsible for recruiting/sourcing marketing and sourcing strategies across many modalities: job fairs, TV, radio, multiple job boards, Facebook, Twitter, LinkedIn, YouTube, Instagram, other digital platforms.
- Tools used: iCiMS, Taleo, Lawson, ADP, Excel, Word, PowerPoint.

COMPANY2, Overland Park, KS
April 2013 – December 2014
Talent Acquisition Specialist
- Responsible for the full lifecycle of recruiting for a healthcare IT company, both locally and nationally.
- Successfully placed over 90 associates in Sales, Marketing (creative/tactical), Product Marketing, Accounting/Finance (revenue recognition), Consulting, Project Managers, Operations, IT (security, support, developers), and Healthcare (Accountable Care, Meaningful Use).

In the first example, you see a variety of fonts, font sizes, and spacing. You can clearly see that the bulleting is not used consistently and there are some spelling errors and inconsistent grammar (missing commas and periods). This may seem like an exaggeration of a bad resume, but I've actually seen a lot worse than this.

Notice that in the second example, everything is uniform, the same font is used and the bolding and bulleting are consistent, making it easy to read and follow where the candidate worked and what was accomplished. You can represent yourself very professionally and cleanly, or you can make yourself look messy, sloppy and lazy.

4. Contact Information

This should be self-explanatory, but do NOT take it for granted. It is very easy to miss something important here. One little typo in your email could mean the difference between getting a phone interview with a company and never hearing back from them.

You may be shocked to learn that about 3-5% of all the resumes I receive are either missing an email address, a phone number or both!

How can a company contact you if you don't provide a means of reaching out? Make sure both your email and phone number are included in your resume, and they are easy to read and conspicuous.

It has now also become a best practice to include a link to your LinkedIn profile in your contact information. More and more hiring managers are asking for this information, so it makes sense to provide that clickable link on your resume to make it easier for a potential employer to get to know you better. Of course, this requires you to have a well-crafted LinkedIn profile that matches up with your resume. I will discuss this in greater detail in Chapter 4.

Email Address

This piece of information is a mandatory, have-to-have on your resume! Most Applicant Tracking Systems (i.e., the database that recruiters use to track candidates through the interviewing and hiring process) use your email address as the unique identifier.

This means that if you don't provide your email address, and I received your resume via email through a referral or other job board, then I have no way to "add" you to my database! This could mean you may never hear from me. Don't make it difficult for recruiters to add you to their system and to contact you.

Many times, recruiters are so overwhelmed with resumes, that we will select a few to contact and send out a quick email to those candidates to get more information or request a phone interview. If you don't have an email in your resume, you won't get that email.

Another concern is applying for an additional position with the same company but using a different email address to create a new account. It's understandable that you may need to change your email address after a long period of time. However, in many Applicant Tracking systems, the recruiter never knows about the earlier application or even previous interviews you had with the company. This sometimes leads to confusion during the screening and interviewing process, especially if you aren't very upfront about that earlier interaction with the company.

Even worse is when you apply for a job using one email, get rejected for whatever reason. You see the job is still posted, so you apply again using the same name and resume, but a different email, causing the recruiter to review and reject again. Please don't do this, it only makes you look bad in the eyes of the employer and reduces your chances of being considered in the relative future.

Also, and this is VERY important, keep your email address "professional"! Email addresses that begin with things like "partygirl@...", "redneckdude@...", momatemysnack@..., or (I've even seen) "demonghostofthewestwood@...", may be fun or funny in your personal life, but they show a side to a hiring manager or recruiter that may not give the best first impression.

The best format or email convention is to use your name. For example, "greg.austin88@mail.com" is simple, professional, and very acceptable. No one can make a negative inference about you, using that format. And let's face it, perception is reality.

You may not be a "party girl" anymore but the employer's perception is "their" reality, and they could make snap judgments to your character or dependability, so don't give them a reason to.

Also, it is very important to use your own email address when corresponding with a potential employer. Some candidates will use a spouse's or boyfriend's or girlfriend's email address. I'm not sure why people do this, but it is very confusing to Corporate Recruiters who will be reviewing your resume and emailing you.

For example, I recently received an email from Angela Smith inquiring about the status of her candidacy and here is how it appeared at the top of my Outlook email:

Angela Smith <angelkisses25@mail.com>

Re: Your Interview

The first thing I did was to search in my Applicant Tracking System (the recruiter's database) to quickly find Angela to check on the notes and view the status of her application. Strangely, I couldn't find her anywhere in my records, which was quite odd, since clearly I had contacted her in the past based on the subject heading.

After doing some more digging, I found that the email address was actually linked to her husband, Derek Smith. Not only did this cause confusion and waste my time in unnecessary work, but also the email address itself does not scream "I'm professional."

It is also wise to use an email provider that has good reputation. Providers such as Yahoo and Hotmail have become unreliable and has thus affected their deliverability. The last thing you want is to miss out on an opportunity because an email didn't arrive as expected in yours or the company's inbox.

Physical Address
If you are uncomfortable about putting your home address in the resume, then you should at least put the city and state that you reside in. If you prefer that level of privacy, that's fine. You can reserve that

information for the application the company will require from you (and they will).

If you are worried about being overlooked because you are not a local candidate, leaving out your location is a terrible strategy.

Some companies will not relocate or wait for a candidate to relocate under "any" circumstance, no matter how good, talented and skilled you are, so it is better etiquette to be upfront with all the facts, including where you live.

Conversely, some companies are happy to pay full relocation expenses for great talent. It all depends on the needs of the company and the budget they have set aside for relocations.

LinkedIn Profile
If you're on LinkedIn, and you most certainly should be (especially in a job hunt), I recommend that you put your LinkedIn web link (URL) in your contact information on your resume.

Hiring managers and executive leaders are now requesting this information anyway, so it's smart to have a strong profile already set up on LinkedIn and give that link to them for easy access. I will provide a brief LinkedIn tutorial in Chapter 4.

Should your Picture be on your Resume?

In a word, "NO." While it may help hiring managers and recruiters remember you by putting a face to the name, it is highly recommended that you don't.

It's best to stay away from any biases or prejudices by the reader. You don't want to broadcast your race, creed, religion, color or age by posting your picture on your resume. This seems to be normal practice for salespeople and some executives, but regardless of the field, I do not recommend it. Let your skills, experience, and accomplishments speak for themselves first!

People naturally look at images before reading text. Sometimes potential employers will look at the picture and make a conscious or subconscious prejudgment before they read one word of your resume. The only exception that seems to stand out is if you are famous or very well-known, such as a CEO for a distinguished and renowned company, then the picture is best used to verify identity.

Professional Summary/Objective Statement or not?

Many job seekers include this at the top of their resume. The question is: Is it necessary or not? The answer is, "No, it's not necessary."

Most hiring managers and recruiters are satisfied with gleaning your professional background and strengths from your Professional Skills summary and your job history. However, if written well, it can be helpful to capture the reader's attention, but it can also be redundant and a waste of good real estate on your resume's front page.

It is highly recommended that the summary or objective statement adds value to the resume in some way, especially if it clarifies your skills as they relate to the job description you are applying for specifically.

> *For example, let's imagine you just applied for a Staff Accounting position and below is the objective statement you wrote:*

OBJECTIVE
To gain secure employment with a good company in their Accounting Department as a Staff Accountant.

Since you just applied for a role as a Staff Accountant, this statement is very redundant. You applied as a Staff Accountant, so I already know that's your next career goal. It then just takes up unnecessary space that could otherwise be used for highlighting your unique skills and accomplishments.

The only utility to this statement is if you are networking and handing your resume (or emailing it) to a friend, colleague or potential hiring manager when you haven't directly applied for a role, so they immediately understand what type of position you are seeking.

It could also be helpful for recent college graduates who have not landed their first "career" job yet and wish to articulate what it is they want to do with their new college degree. While the latter 2 statements are true, it can still be worded in a much better way to get an employer's attention and start off with a more remarkable first impression.

Let's take a look at a much better approach:

PROFESSIONAL SUMMARY
Results-oriented, degreed accountant with strong work ethic and over 2 years of experience. Team-oriented professional who prepares clear, comprehensive financial reports for executive-level management. Seeking entry-level staff accountant position with room for growth.

Can you see how much more professional that sounds? The second example demonstrates someone who is sharp, tenacious, ready to tackle professional accounting projects, to not only get the necessary work done but can also make the Accounting Manager (their boss) look good. That kind of an impression can lead to an interview, which as I mentioned is the whole point of the resume.

5. Professional Skills & Accomplishments

This is a crucial section to put at or near the top of your resume to highlight your key skills and accomplishments. It is what makes you stand out and shine above other candidates. This section should be a very conspicuous, bulleted list with short statements.

I believe this is a mandatory section. The purpose of this section is to get the potential employer to continue reading and strongly desire to read through your entire job history, even if it's a long one.

After already reading through many resumes, recruiters and hiring managers alike can get fatigued, but if the first thing they see are those required skill sets that they need, they get a boost of energy and excitement, that they finally found a valid candidate for their position. Now, they really want to read on to see if you truly are a potential fit.

There are many positions out there that are quite specific, and the employer really *needs* a particular skill set for a critical company function to operate well.

It could be a salesperson with specific sales or technical experience or degree. It could be an IT professional with expertise in a less common programming language, or simply a technician who loves to travel for a position that is 90% on the road.

CUSTOMIZE YOUR ACCOMPLISHMENTS

These skills and accomplishments should, first of all, highlight the best you have to offer and anything that could make you stand out to any employer. However, and this is VERY important, you should **customize** this part of your resume especially to the key needs or qualifications that you find in the job description.

These are usually critical needs for the company, and if you have exactly what they need, or at least fairly close, then it is absolutely in your best interest to *customize* your resume to the job description. If you are taking *the shotgun* approach in your job search, then you may be thinking, "If I customize every resume before I apply, then it will take forever, and I may miss out on new job openings because I'm taking so long to customize for these other jobs!"

In fact, you may be right. If you are urgently seeking employment and wish to shotgun your resume to many employers, then you should only send a customized resume to those targeted employers whom you are particularly excited about. But, if you use this approach, you greatly increase your chances of getting a call, especially for those recruiters and hiring managers who are resume "skimmers".

Key Technique for Customizing Your Resume

I highly recommend that before customizing your resume to a job description that you first create a long-version of your resume to be used for creating custom resumes and as an interview guide. I call this your Master Resume Template

To create this template, first, write down in your resume, everything you can possibly think of that you did for each position. Write each duty and responsibility, no matter how small, and every accomplishment you can recall. This will be your template or guide from which you can easily build custom resumes. Then, you can put the job description to which you are applying to next to your Master Resume Template and cut out what isn't needed or important in the job description. Then, rearrange what is most important in the job description to show as the "first" bullet point under the job at which you did that particular job duty.

The additional benefit to this exercise is that you have a very detailed historical document to refer to during an interview. This is especially helpful during a phone interview when you can refer to and look at your Master Resume Template while in the interview itself. It is also a good study tool while preparing for onsite interviews.

Note: You should always be updating your resume in real time, for each new accomplishment, as it happens. For example, if you're responsible for new dynamic content in your company's website that helped them market a particular project, write it down that night after work and put it in your resume. You never know when your company will sell, lay off, etc., so you want to be prepared with everything you've done, so that you get generate a good resume quickly. It's very difficult to recall these small but significant accomplishments years later, so write it down while it's still fresh.

Let's take a look at the requirements of a particular job description and a couple of examples to demonstrate how effective this approach can be:

Job Description:
SALES ENGINEER/MANAGER – INDUSTRIAL SALES

Job Requirements

- **College degree in Engineering (Mechanical, Civil, Chemical, Electrical, Industrial).**

- A background that includes knowledge of pumping, waste-water treatment, biological treatment systems, headworks, electrical control systems or other capital equipment.

- Experience in Engineering, working for a Manufacturer, or a Manufacturer's Rep firm, is highly preferred.

- Minimum 5 years' experience in Sales calls, negotiations, closing business.

- The ability to work with and communicate with a variety of people in a positive, persuasive and professional manner is critical.

- Ability to travel 50-75% is required.

As you can see, this company needs a degreed engineer with strong sales experience in the wastewater industry, who is able to travel quite a bit to be successful. See below for a solid example of a Professional Expertise section that would inspire a recruiter to pick up the phone right away:

PROFESSIONAL EXPERTISE
- Accomplished Technical Sales Engineer with 8 years of Sales Success
- Demonstrated Expertise in the Oil & Gas and Water Treatment Industries
- Strong Technical Background in Chemical Engineering
- Bilingual Professional Skilled at Communicating Design and Deployment of Customer Solutions
- Consultative Business Partner with a Record of Sales Success
- Sold $800K in business in 2017
- Willing to Travel up to 75%

These are actual points of expertise that speak directly to the needs of the business of the employer. I would call this person immediately!!

Unfortunately, I don't see this approach very often, so it is a clear opportunity for you to stand out if you follow this method.

If you hold any "preferred" or "required" certifications as per the job description that makes you more competitive in your field, then it's a good idea to mention them in this section. This is especially important for IT professionals to list their certifications and programming languages.

Accomplishments

Anytime you can "quantify" what you have accomplished, speaks volumes about how you can quickly bring a positive impact to a prospective employer. For example, list out precisely how much in revenue you sold ($800K in 2017), or how much money you saved the company ($200K in 2017), or anything else that you accomplished, particularly if it is easily quantifiable:

- Successfully implemented JD Edwards software in 2017
- Hired 56 new professionals in 2016
- Implemented a new Learning Management System in 2014, etc.

It's a good idea to put a date or time frame to it so that the hiring manager knows when it happened. Even if it's an older accomplishment, you might as well date it, because they are likely going to ask for those details during the interview.

It is perfectly fine to repeat those accomplishments in the Professional Experience section of your resume, so they know precisely when and where you made a difference. In fact, I recommend you do this.

DO NOT embellish or exaggerate your accomplishments!! It's far better to list a minor accomplishment, then get caught in a lie. You never know who knows who in this world, and it is indeed a small world.

Perhaps you share on your resume that you saved an employer $200,000 by something you did, when in reality you only saved them $80,000. You decided to inflate the number to make yourself look more valuable. What you didn't know is that the person now reading your resume personally knows your old boss and calls him to corroborate only to find out that you greatly exaggerated your accomplishment.

This kind of practice will ruin trust and mar your integrity. Just don't do it. This goes for anything in your resume whether under Skills, Experience, Education, etc.

6. Education and Certifications

There is a debate in the recruiting industry about whether education should appear before or after your "Professional Experience." In my professional opinion, "it depends." It is sometimes difficult to know how important having a degree, or specific degree is to a hiring manager, but there are some clues.

Having a college degree may not be as important if it states in the job description that a degree is "preferred" or if it states "Bachelor's degree or relevant experience."
Keep in mind that a candidate with a college degree is usually preferred, but not always necessary. However, if the job description asks for a specific degree in "Chemical Engineering" or "Medicinal Chemistry", etc., then you can bet that if you do not possess the necessary degree, then you will very likely NOT be considered.

If that's the case, it's really not worth your time to apply. It could even tarnish your image if you apply for a position you are clearly not qualified for (but think maybe you can do it), then also apply for another position in the company.

The employer may get annoyed that you wasted their time to begin with, by applying for something you were not qualified to do; and may be less willing to consider you for another position that you are better suited for.

Believe me, being a "fast learner" is fine and good, but it does not make up for lacking a particular degree (especially a technical one) or years of experience in a particular area. I hear this a lot in the interview process from candidates who think that their presumed learning ability can make up for any deficits in their education or experience. In reality, we rarely hire someone in this circumstance.

If the degree appears to be required, then go ahead and put it after your Professional Skills and Accomplishments and before your Professional Experience. It's usually the first thing we look for to identify relevant candidates and the easier we can find what we need, the faster we will call you. Resist the urge of placing it at the bottom of your resume.

Be very clear in stating what your education actually is. Don't leave the employer wondering what degree you have.

Bad Example:

Bachelor's Degree, U. of Maryland.

A bachelor's degree in what? Even if the job requires "any" kind of bachelor's degree, we always want to know in what field you studied.

As you've undoubtedly seen, many job descriptions out there are pretty weak, so you don't know what they really value the most with regards to your education or background. Be specific! Maybe they would love to see a Marketing degree or a degree from a specific school.

Below is a clearer example:

Good Example:

B.A. Marketing, University of Maryland, 2010

If you don't possess the "preferred" degree, but you do have relevant experience, then go ahead and mention that just below the education that you do have to keep the hiring manager's or recruiter's attention:

Experience over degree example:

o   A.A. Business Administration, Johnson County Community College, 2004
    ▪   (10 years' experience of industrial sales in the Chemical Industry)

For certifications, the same basic rules apply. If you possess a certification that is preferred or required, then make it "very" apparent to the reader. As previously mentioned, you should put them in your Professional Skills section if you are going to list

Education and Certifications at the bottom of your resume.

Make sure your certifications stand out, <u>especially</u> if they are mentioned in the job description of the position you are applying for.

7. Professional Experience
This is clearly the most important section of your resume! This will tell us if you can potentially do what is needed to help the company accomplish its goals and mission.

As I mentioned earlier in the Basic Formatting section of this book, it is critically important to have good formatting that flows well and is easy to follow all the stops in your career as well as what you have accomplished, what you were responsible for and who you managed (if applicable).

Also, be sure to include a quick statement or bullet point on what your company does or at least which industry the company operated in. This gives quick insights to the recruiter for matching industry knowledge and experience to any particular role!

Many of us have one or more short stops or bad blips on our resume. This could have been through no fault of your own (i.e., your company suddenly sold and laid everyone off) or perhaps a bad decision on your part.

If you have one or more of these, it's important to handle it properly in your resume to shed the best light on a bad situation.

Let me share a true story with you. I worked with a candidate who had a pretty solid background in what we needed, but his most recent job seemed confusing. He mentioned 2 different companies with very little detail about them. Here is what it looked like:

PROFESSIONAL EXPERIENCE

Brody Trucking Co./OPP Transportation KCKS/KSMO 2016-2018

City and OTR Trucking Companies

Dispatcher

Handled city and OTR dispatch as well as all sales and billing.

I am a very thorough Recruiter, so when I screen a candidate, I'm going to dig into each position you've held, what you did and why you left. When I screened this candidate, it was in the first week of January 2018, so my first question was, "Are you still working there?" He told me "no" which confused me since it had just become 2018.

Then he advised that he parted ways with OPP in June of 2017. Since he put down 2018 and it had only been 2018 for a couple of days, I assumed that he was still there. Imagine my surprise that he'd been out of work for 6 months (Red flag #1).

Then I asked him if he worked for both companies simultaneously (sometimes that happens). He advised no and that he was several months at one company, then a few months at the other (Red flag #2).

He then explained that both companies were experiencing difficult financial situations, mostly because of their poor procedures and though he tried to help them, it didn't work out.

He was clearly embarrassed by this and by having to explain what had actually happened. He continued on and explained that a friend of his paid an agency recruiter to help him with his resume. Agency recruiters don't work to fill positions for a company they work for directly, but act as a 3rd party recruiter, helping place candidates in different client companies for a fee. It is highly unusual for an agency recruiter to both take money from companies to place good candidates there AND to take money from candidates to help them improve their chances. It is generally considered unethical business practice even if they keep parties separate.

This recruiter told him those 2 positions didn't look good for only a few months each.   The recruiter further advised him to combine the positions to make him look more attractive and less like a job jumper.

Unfortunately for him, this was terrible advice, and while it may have briefly looked better on paper, once I dug deeper it made him look dishonest. If you're taking advice, even from a seasoned and experienced recruiter, make sure it lines up with good and honest business practices. If it doesn't, then just don't do it!

This may seem like obvious advice and it should, but if you don't read up on it or spend a good amount of time in the job market, these concepts may not be so straightforward. For instance, this candidate had previously been a Vice President for two other companies and was likely at least a fairly sharp and wise person. He just took bad advice from a "so-called" expert in the field of recruiting.

If you have short stops in your job history, there are ways to make it look better on paper, but you have to be honest and accurate. What typically helps the most is to quickly explain your reason for leaving just under the job title and company. Some good reasons to share would be: "Relocated", "Company went out of business", "Company lost contracts, laid off", etc.

For example, this would work much better:

PROFESSIONAL EXPERIENCE

Brody Trucking Co., Kansas City, KS
1/2017 – 6/2017
Dispatcher/Sales Agent
(Reason for leaving: Company lost 3 major contracts, laid off)

- Managed city and OTR dispatching.
- Conducted cold calls to generate new business.
- Sold $6,000 in new business.
- Billed customers and collected on debts.

OPP Transportation, Gladstone, MO
3/2016 – 11/2016
Sales Agent
(Reason for leaving: Company under investigation by government, resigned)

- Conducted cold calls to generate new business.
- Aligned best carrier and preferred pricing to customers' needs

Now that I've covered some of the basics, I'll discuss some good tips and hacks to make your job history firmly stand out to a recruiter or hiring manager. Earlier in this book, I mentioned the need to use very clear, easy to read formatting. That idea is paramount in this section.

The last thing you want to do is make it confusing or difficult for the reader to ascertain if you have what they need, or just make it hard on the eyes to read.

43

It is imperative that your job history is clear.

You should state plainly:
- where you worked
- what the dates of employment were
  - (be as accurate as possible)
- what your title was
- what your responsibilities were
- what you accomplished
  - Be specific and quantify it!

This section is the meat of your resume and will tell prospective employers if you have the requisite skills and experience to be considered for their needs. You are marketing yourself, and you must demonstrate your value to them, or they will never call.

As I mentioned before, you should bold your company name, location, dates of employment on the first line, then your job title on the next line. The rest should be a bulleted list of your job responsibilities and accomplishments.

The accomplishments are particularly important as they go beyond showing what you were required to do in the job, but what "impact" you had, especially if the accomplishments went above and beyond your job description and perhaps led to a company award or promotion.

This is critical because it will demonstrate to the employer that you are dedicated to helping the business grow and thrive, that's absolutely what they really want!!

Exercise:
1. Get out a piece of paper or open up a Word document.
2. For each job that you've worked in, think of what you accomplished.
    a. It could be you saved the company money, you led a team through a successful project, you increased revenue for the company, you improved a process, etc.
3. Quantify as best you can, the impact of the accomplishment.
    a. For example, you saved the company $100,000 in 2015 (explain how but be brief).
    b. You increased revenue by $50,000 in 2016.
    c. You streamlined a process reducing the time to complete from 3 weeks to 5 days, etc.
4. Add these bullets to your resume under the jobs during which you completed them.
5. Also, add to your Professional Accomplishments section at the top of your resume as appropriate.
    d. List the most impactful ones, not every single accomplishment.

Take a look at this example from my own resume:

COMPANY1, Hamilton, OH January 2015 – June 2017
Recruiting Manager

- Responsible for the full lifecycle of recruiting for a local call center and corporate recruiting roles.
- Hired 618 new employees in 2016 in the customer service industry.
- Led a team of 3 in the recruiting department.
- Responsible for recruiting/sourcing marketing and sourcing strategies across many modalities: job fairs, TV, radio, multiple job boards, Facebook, Twitter, LinkedIn, YouTube, Instagram, other digital platforms.
- Conducted 6 onsite Job Fair events successfully in 2016 resulting in 63 hires.
- Tools used: iCiMS, Taleo, Lawson, ADP, Excel, Word, PowerPoint.

In this example, you can clearly see where I worked, when I worked, and what my title was. In the first two bullet points, you can clearly see what my primary responsibilities were and what my accomplishments were during my tenure at that company. You know that I dealt with a large volume of hiring, 618 hires in one year is a lot!

Also, I successfully executed 6 onsite job fair events that resulted in 63 hires and during which time period

(1 year) it took to do it. These show very clear, quantifiable results, so any hiring manager looking for effective, fast-paced, high volume recruiting would be very interested to see this.

If the job description for the position I was applying for, stated clearly, they needed high-volume recruiting and innovative recruiting solutions, then I would move those accomplishments to my first 2 bullets, so they stand out and get read first.

Align Your Abilities and Accomplishments Directly to the Needs in the Job Description

The absolute worst thing you can do is to leave out a key achievement or skill you have that is directly related and clearly needed by the company you are applying to.

Yes, it takes more time to adjust or edit your resume to these positions, and it's true, they may never call you, but you never know when that one key skill is the one thing that sticks out and gets the recruiter's attention which then leads to a call.

But if you leave it out for whatever reason, you are reducing your chances. It's all about marketing yourself, and that involves communicating your value to the future employer. It's the same for a product you may or may not want. If the company doesn't communicate the value of the product to you in some way, then why would you buy it?

Addressing Gaps in Your Resume

I get a lot of questions about how to handle this issue. Many people have gaps of some kind in their resume. It could be you had a baby and stayed home for a period of time, you left the workforce to care for an ailing parent, you got laid off because the company downsized and it took 4 months to find another good fit, or perhaps you had a serious illness or a surgery.

I've listened to all kinds of reasons during my hundreds of phone screens with candidates. I've heard about sabbaticals, jail time and losing a baby which led to a gap. You want to address it up front and be as transparent as is appropriate.

Clearly, some gaps are easily explainable and perfectly acceptable, particularly the aforementioned time off for a baby or taking care of a parent. For these cases, you can actually write it into your job description as if it were a job.

For example:

Henderson, LLC   **09/2011 – 05/2014**
PBX Operator
- Operate PBX or private branch exchange switchboards to facilitate connections, take and relay messages.
- Manage busy switchboard for businesses and direct outgoing, interoffice or incoming calls.
- Service a high volume of calls managing a diverse customer base.

Homemaker   **02/2009 – 09/2011**
- Cared for a newborn and managed all aspects of a busy household.

Everette Corp Conference Division
07/1999 – 02/2009
Conference Agent
- Reserve and coordinate business conference calls in a timely and accurate manner.
- Technical Operation of Sprint System 70, Keyboarding Skills, Fax, Calculator/Adding.
- Offer superior customer service to all parties and ensure conferencing meets customers guidelines.
- Process and assist in all requests before and during conference calls on all platforms.

Conversely, you could simply state your reason for a gap:

Gap – Cared for an ailing family member full time. **05/2003 – 06/2005**

In either case, this method makes it very clear exactly why and how long you were in between jobs.

Those are the easy cases. What if the reason for the time between positions is not so pretty? For these situations, I suggest you stay sincere but choose your words very carefully. Many people work with, work for, or otherwise help out family in some way (in their business, on their farm, etc.) while they are looking for a new position. In these cases, you can state in the gap period that you assisted with the family business.

If your gap is due to a personal crisis, whether it is emotional, physical, or the result of a very poor decision, I don't suggest being detailed about those reasons on a resume. For example, if you went through a divorce, the death of a loved one or another personal crisis, do not state that in the resume.

Rather than leaving it as a blank gap in the resume (which will get questioned by a recruiter or hiring manager), go ahead and address it up front, but keep it vague. You can go into more detail during an interview. You could call it a "Personal Sabbatical" with the date ranges.

For example:

Personal Sabbatical   **05/2003 – 06/2005**

This way the recruiter will know that you're not trying to "gloss over" that gap in your employment history which can then be explained if you get an interview or a phone screen. You can mention some of those reasons in the interview, but don't go into too much detail, please! We don't want to hear too much of that story, and frankly, it could cause you harm in the hiring process if someone misperceives something you say and decide not to move forward with you.

For example, if you went through a divorce, you can simply state: "I went through a difficult divorce during that time, which took a lot of my attention away from my professional life. Fortunately, I was able to take some personal time off to get through that rough spot, get my head straight, so that I could be at my best in my next job."

This is a very professional and acceptable way of explaining it, without going into gruesome detail about how your spouse broke things, took the house and the dog and your kids wouldn't talk to you for a while, and how it really messed you up, but you're okay now! That's personal information, so keep it that way.

If you had a medical procedure or injury that took you out of work, you are protected by law that you do not have to go into detail about the nature of the illness, injury or procedure. You can simply state that you took time off to recover from a medical problem and that you are now healthy and ready to work.

If you spent time in jail, it's best to just come clean about the charges and the time served. You don't need to go into detail about what you did but be very aware that any employer who runs a criminal background check, and many do, will find out anyway. If you try to be too sneaky about it and they find out, it just makes you appear dishonest. This kind of information is best during an interview, I do not recommend putting that on your resume.

That being said, it would behoove you to check into the state laws regarding how far back in years a company can go to check into the criminal background of a candidate. Some states only allow 7 years, some 10 years, others have no restrictions and they can go back until you were 18. This means, if you were convicted of something many years ago that would not show up on a background check, then there is no need to disclose that up front.

Addressing Multiple Positions in One Company

It is important and helpful to go over all the positions you have held within a single company, but you should be careful about how you write it on your resume.

You want to make it very clear up front that you spent a long period of time at the one company and had multiple roles within it. If you're not clear about that, then it could appear to the reader that rather than showing strong job history of 7 years with an employer, it instead seems that you hopped around 4 times quickly.

The keen reader should pick this out, but in the reality of recruiting, when recruiters are experiencing resume reading fatigue and under pressure to find suitable candidates quickly, they sometimes miss those details at first.

Your job is to make the essential facts of your job history stand out well and improve the readability of your resume so that it reduces the chances the reader misses something important. You also want to clearly emphasize any promotions you earned along the way.

Let me illustrate. Below is an example in which the candidate lists each position within the same company individually, but never overtly states the entire time the candidate spent at the company:

Sales Manager, ACME Engineered Systems, (Sept 2011 to May 2016)
- Manage Department of 8 direct reports: Proposal Managers & Sale Engineers
- Primary contact for all domestic and international manufacturers
- Review all estimates, proposals and T&C's for all contracts
- Set profit margins (within specified ranges) to support shop loading and company profit goals
- Developed training program and manual for new Sales Department hires

Sales Engineer, ACME Engineered Systems, (Sept 2010 to Sept 2011)
- Responsible for developing and growing sales in North American territory not covered by reps
- Growth, development, and expansion of assigned territory. (50% growth over previous 6 years)

Proposal Manager, ACME Engineered Systems, (Sept 2007 to Sept 2010)
- Responsible for writing out bills of material for incoming projects
- Worked closely with customers to properly spec out and bid projects

While the candidate does include the same company name for each position since the job title comes first, the company name may not stick out, and at first glance, the candidate seems to have jumped around a bit, when indeed the candidate was with ACME for 9 years, which is far more impressive.

Below is a clearer method for writing this section:

ACME Engineered Systems (2007 – 2016)
   Sales Manager, ACME Engineered Systems, (Sept 2011 to May 2016)
   - Manage Department of 8 direct reports: Proposal Managers & Sale Engineers.
   - Primary contact for all domestic and international manufacturers.
   - Review all estimates, proposals and T&C's for all contracts.
   - Set profit margins (within specified ranges) to support shop loading and company profit goals.
   - Developed training program and manual for new Sales Department hires.

   Sales Engineer, ACME Engineered Systems, (Sept 2010 to Sept 2011)
   - Responsible for developing and growing sales in North American territory not covered by reps.

- Growth, development, and expansion of assigned territory. (50% growth achieved)
- Promoted to Sales Manager based on performance and leadership abilities demonstrated.

Proposal Manager, ACME Engineered Systems, (Sept 2007 to Sept 2010)
- Responsible for writing out bills of material for incoming projects.
- Worked closely with customers to properly spec out and bid projects.
- Promoted to Sales Engineer based on strong performance and dedication.

As you can see, the 9 years of service at ACME clearly stands out, and we added bullet points to the Sales Engineer and Proposal Manager positions to show the promotions and career advancement.

How Many Years Back Do You Go in your Job History?
This is another important question that comes up often. The honest answer to this question is, "it depends." What it depends upon is how many years of work history you have and determining if going back beyond 10 or 15 years will help you land an interview for that position.

For example, if you have 20 years of experience in Accounting and the position you are applying for is

Controller, then you should go all the way back to show your breadth of experience in the field.

However, if you spent the first 10 years in a sales position, then the last 10 years in Accounting, then it's okay just to go back the first 10 years. If the recruiter or hiring manager wants to know more, then you can fill them in at the interview stage.

The risk in going back too far is that it gives insight to your age and unfortunately age discrimination happens. If you do decide to leave out a portion of your job history, then I strenuously recommend that you leave OFF the dates to your education.

If the dates are on there, then they can quickly calculate your age. Many companies value experience and wisdom, but some don't, so it is prudent to protect yourself in this way.

8. Awards, Patents, Publications
These should appear below your job history and should be relevant to your professional accomplishments. Awards can demonstrate career achievements and should not be left out.

For example, the President's award for sales which included a trip to Tahiti, Employee Contributor of the Year, or Sales Person of the Month are all excellent accolades you want the potential employer to know about. Whatever they are, list them as bullet points by name and date (year only is fine), and you can add a short descriptor in parentheses or in a lower bullet point to describe what the significance of the award was and what you did to achieve it.

Stay consistent with the formatting, and it is also a good idea to mention some or all of the awards in your job history as appropriate.

I do not recommend listing many personal awards unless they are relevant and impressive. For example, I see a lot of mentions for attaining Eagle Scout level, which is a long, arduous process, so it demonstrates hard work and deep commitment. However, no one probably cares if you won the Derby Race in 5th grade, so avoid going too far in the past and keep it relevant.

Patents and publications are self-explanatory and are typically more relevant to positions in academia. However, if you have patents, it is very important to list them in your job history and can be mentioned again in a 'Patents' or 'Publications' section after your job history. It is important to list them in your job history because it provides a quick reference point in time to that achievement and keeps it very relatable to that part of your job history.

In a resume, contrary to a CV (curriculum vitae), you should keep your patent or publication information brief.

For example:

> "Awarded 3 patents for product design improvements at ACME, Inc."

You can go into further detail about your patents in the interview if asked and you can bring extra documentation to list out your patents and publications as well.

In some cases, depending upon the job description, you may want to list them out in detail, but if you do have a lot of patents, it can make your resume unnecessarily long if it's not as directly relevant to the job you are applying for. The same goes for publications.

9. Volunteer Work, Personal Interests and Hobbies
You should always include your volunteer work on your resume. It demonstrates your character and willingness to give back to the community and contribute.

If your volunteer experience is very lengthy, then I suggest you only keep the top 5 experiences that are most important to you, including one that is the most recent.

For example:

VOLUNTEER WORK and OTHER ACTIVITIES

- SHRM of Johnson County, 2014-2015 - Director of Marketing, Board of Directors
- SHRM of Johnson County, 2011-2014 - Membership Committee, Marketing Committee
- Hospice Home, 2012-2013 - Cooked and served Thanksgiving and Christmas meals
- St. Paul's Episcopal Church, 2012 – served food to the needy
- Amendment 21 (Band), 2012-2015, Lead Singer/Rhythm Guitar

As you can see, I included my professional association volunteer work which is relevant to my field, my community contributions, and my hobby.

The volunteer work, personal interests, and hobbies are conversation starters and give insight into the character and personality of the candidate.

CHAPTER 2:

PROOFREAD, PROOFREAD, PROOFREAD!!!

More resumes have ended up in the trash can because of a simple spelling error than you care to know about. There are numerous hiring managers out there that put so much value on spelling, grammar, detail orientation, and format, that if a resume has any errors on it or is poorly formatted, then it can quickly get tossed in the garbage or will drop your ranking amongst other candidates very quickly.

Can you really blame them? Your resume is your calling card it is your brand! Should your brand tell the world that you are sloppy, lazy and incapable of spelling properly?? NO!! Especially in this day and age of auto-spell checkers and grammar checking software. There really is no excuse for it.

Today's latest spelling and grammar technologies make it much easier than it used to be to spot and fix errors quickly and efficiently. Microsoft Word has automated spell checking and some minor grammar checking.

The Grammarly plug-in to Microsoft Word and for Google Chrome is available for free download.

Just look for it online or you can use this link to access Grammarly directly:

https://grammarly.go2cloud.org/SH1UJ

From the main page, you can easily click to add to Google Chrome, which frankly is helpful anytime you're using online Google Docs to write your resume, online email programs, posting on any social media, or for blogging. It will check spelling and grammar and provide good examples to correct mistakes or typos.

If you scroll to the bottom of the page, you will find a link on the bottom left area for a link to the free download for MS Word. The paid version will get into more technical grammar help, but it's not something you would need for a resume, only more serious writing. The spelling and basic grammar checking will quickly and easily spot errors and provide a quick click to fixing the error. I use it myself in many areas.

You should read your resume over 3 times slowly. It is easy to overlook simple mistakes that a grammar or spell check may miss because you've looked at it so much. Therefore, it's very necessary to take your time, read it out loud so you hear every word which will make it much easier to hear and see the mistakes on the page. Then, make the necessary corrections and send it to a trusted friend or colleague to review it for errors. After any errors have been fixed, then ask them if the format and language is easy to read and very clear BEFORE you post it on a job board like Indeed, Career Builder, Monster, etc. and definitely before you submit it to a prospective employer.

Ask them for direct and blunt feedback, then suck up your pride, listen to their advice, and act on it as appropriate. Sometimes another's opinions do not seem to make sense. If that's the case, then get 2-3 more opinions on it to be sure. They are trying to help you get your next job, so let them, and under NO circumstances should you skip this step!!

CHAPTER 3:
USING JOB BOARDS, BEST PRACTICES

There are now dozens of job boards available online and they all have their own rules and interfaces. These job boards have their own pros and cons. I will review some of the tips and pitfalls of using some of the top ones out there today.

One overriding rule that fits for using any of these job boards is if you upload your resume, make sure it is the best version of your resume, it's completely up to date, and that it fits the formatting convention of that particular job board.

Outdated versions of your resume will only cause confusion with recruiters and hiring managers reviewing your credentials who assume you have the latest and the greatest version posted. Some job boards, like Indeed, will force you into their own formatting rules. More on Indeed in a moment.

Zip Recruiter
This has become a very popular job board that is widely used today. The reason it's so popular is that you can use the downloadable app on your phone to easily search for posted jobs and apply to them. After you have uploaded your resume online, Zip Recruiter will look for related job titles posted by companies and notify you directly on the app and via email.

Sometimes employers will pay to have their job post boosted to candidates in a geographic area with certain keywords in their resume or on their account. Then you can simply swipe to apply to many of the positions out there which very quickly sends your resume and a very basic application to the employer.

This sounds great, right? Not so much for the Corporate Recruiter receiving your resume. This is because, instead of your resume going directly into the Applicant Tracking System (ATS – also known as the recruiter's resume database), the recruiter will have to load each resume manually, which can be very time-consuming.

Further, if you're not at all qualified for the position, which was so easy for you apply to, it becomes very frustrating and time consuming for the recruiter to sift through many additional resumes which may be irrelevant to the position. My company discontinued using Zip Recruiter for this reason. We did receive a large volume of resumes, but so many of them were not qualified for the position and thus became background noise. In essence, it became a huge waste of time since the vast majority of the applicants would never even make it to the phone screen stage of the evaluation process.

This takes us back to the earlier discussion of the Shotgun vs. Targeted approach to your job search. If you feel the need to shotgun your resume to many employers, please be sure you at least meet the minimum requirements or can easily justify a lack of 1-2 job requirements with your work experience.

Some employers (perhaps most of them) will redirect you to their Careers Page and require you to apply online through their website. This can be frustrating at times for candidates, especially when the online application process is very long (20+ minutes to complete)! I know, I have been there many times myself. However, most employers are getting better at streamlining the application process, thus shortening the time commitment to apply and improving the candidate experience.

Be aware that may also be a test! Employers want to know if you're serious enough to spend at least 5-10 minutes of your day applying to work at their company. Anyone can swipe to apply to 10 companies in 2 minutes, but it doesn't demonstrate any real interest or commitment. The converse side of this argument is that you may spend 30 minutes applying to a great company, do your research on them, and really have a strong interest in the role and the corporate culture, only to never hear back from them!

Not even a token "Thank you for applying but we filled the position" email to at least offer some basic closure on the matter.

Frankly, many Corporate Recruiters stink at this. It's sad, but true. And while in many cases they are overworked and stressed out to fill these difficult to fill positions as quickly as possible. Doing a quick "select all resumes" and sending out an email template really isn't that difficult or time consuming.

I have mentioned this several times in my LinkedIn posts to encourage recruiters to improve their candidate communication frequency and quality. Sadly, they are only hurting themselves because candidates remember those companies who will be more caring and communicate appropriately versus those who ghost on them.

Ironically, many of those same recruiters then complain about candidates ghosting on them.

The moral of the story here is, don't fall into the temptation of applying to every position that Zip Recruiter sends you unless you are truly interested in the role and you are truly qualified to do the job. Otherwise, you are simply wasting the recruiter's time and your time in the long run.

Even if you are desperate for a job, if you waste time applying for or even have a phone screen for a position that is clearly not a fit, then you are taking time away from applying to jobs that really do matter to you!

Indeed and Indeed Mobile

Indeed Mobile has a very similar process that is used by Zip Recruiter. It's fast, easy, and can be done right on your Smart Phone. Again, in some ways it is a great way to get your resume out their quickly and get you moving in the hiring process faster, but the same rules that apply to using Zip Recruiter most certainly apply to Indeed Mobile.

That is, apply for positions that truly are a fit and that you meet the minimum qualifications for. Indeed has grown to be currently the largest job board available, since its algorithms are able to scrape job postings from hundreds of careers pages and locations on the internet.

CAUTION: Be advised that if you use Indeed online or via the mobile app, you "need to know" that when you upload your resume, Indeed automatically converts it to their own, uniform style. This can cause multiple formatting problems and confusion on their converted version of your resume.

I have seen it cause multiple errors in the dates of employment on resumes, causing much confusion around candidates' work history and experience. The process has also been known to cause errors on the date of the candidate's education and may even cut out work history completely or leave off the name of a company you worked for.

Be sure to double check this and manually adjust the Indeed version of your resume BEFORE employers see it!

Indeed defends this practice by stating that it helps keep the resumes that recruiters review uniform and easy to read. While this is true, it does a lot more damage than good in my opinion. The tragic part is that if your resume has special formatting in MS Word, then, as previously stated, Indeed will remove the formatting and may completely butcher your job history.

When I have run into this problem myself, as a recruiter, I typically have to sort out discrepancies on the Indeed version of a candidate's resumes during the phone screen process with the candidate. I then ask for a clean copy of their resume which just delays the process and creates extra, unnecessary work for the candidate. It also takes away from the formatting skills and creativity that the candidate might have otherwise shown.

I've complained directly to Indeed about this, as a paying customer who boosts a lot of jobs with them, but I just get back the typical "Big Corporate" propaganda and marketing speak from them. Moral of the story here is when you upload your resume to Indeed, make sure you double check and triple check it for accuracy.

Do NOT trust their resume parsing process! You may have to convert your resume to a text-only version without the formatting for it to upload properly. Also, another way to "avoid" sending the Indeed version of your resume is when you find a job you want to apply to, then search for that company online, go to their careers page and apply directly, where you can upload your resume in its original formatting.

Career Builder/Monster
These are 2 very similar and still somewhat large players in the job board market that allow candidates to post their resumes for free and search for open jobs.

They aren't as prevalent as they once were. Indeed is by far the new favorite, but they can still be useful in terms of finding open jobs and shouldn't be ignored.

If you are in dire need of a job, you should absolutely upload your resume to both of these sites (as well as Indeed and Zip Recruiter) as companies typically purchase access to at least one if not all sites to access and search for candidates on their vast resume databases.

The good news is that neither Career Builder nor Monster will make any formatting changes to your resume. It will be loaded into the system as-is.

Facebook

Facebook has tried to enter the job board market with poor results. Their company page model is typically used for corporate branding and marketing as well as posting for lower paying positions. Higher level positions just do not typically get much of a response rate on this platform.

Some companies will post jobs on their corporate Facebook pages, but it's really a better tool for gaining some insight into the company's culture and how they engage with customers and job seekers. There are now many Job Seeker Groups for each major city and some groups for smaller communities.

These are forums that recruiters and employers will use to post positions and for candidates to post what type of work they're looking for. It is a good idea to join these local groups to hear more about new openings and get a feel for the local job market.

You may be able to get the attention of recruiters who monitor these sites if you create an eye-catching post of what work you can do and what your availability is.

The job economy in each city can vary greatly between each other, and any given city may be flourishing in a bad economy or floundering in a good one. Just because the job economy is good on the average nationwide, it could be terrible in specific areas, or vice-versa.

LinkedIn

LinkedIn is another huge source of job postings, over 10 million globally to be precise. If you have a profile registered with them, then you can click on the "Jobs" button on the top menu to see what jobs are available.

There is an option to run a keyword search by location, and the landing page should show you a section on "Jobs you may be interested in" that will prioritize those positions based on your career interests. LinkedIn allows you to modify your interests at any time and uses a conspicuous link on the page, so it should be easy to find. If you have any trouble, LinkedIn has a useful help page.

In this section, you can optimize the recommended jobs by Job Titles, Locations, Type of Work (full-time, part-time, remote, etc.), Preferred Industries, and Company Size. There is also an option to allow LinkedIn to share with Recruiters that you are open to new opportunities.

Employers cannot see this unless they have purchased LinkedIn Recruiter (a very expensive recruiting tool). LinkedIn keeps it private that you are open to new opportunities but cannot guarantee 100% privacy on this so you may want to be careful if you are conducting a confidential job search.

The good news is, only those with a LinkedIn Recruiter software license (i.e., recruiters using the tool to search for candidates) should be able to know that you are "open to new opportunities." Hiring managers typically do not have access to this.

LinkedIn will also track your saved jobs and jobs you've applied to. You may also choose to purchase a Premium subscription, which will also help you become more visible in general on LinkedIn and to employers. With that service, the jobs section will display the "Jobs where you're a top applicant" on the top of the page, which can be a helpful feature.

The Premium subscription also allows you to see more of who specifically has viewed your profile, which may be nice to know if recruiters are checking you out. It also gives you a number of free LinkedIn

Stellar Resume Writing

messages that you can use to contact others who are not a First Connection to you.

If you don't have a LinkedIn profile, then I strongly urge you to set one up! In fact, stop reading this book right now, grab your resume as a guide, and create a profile this moment!!! Google "How to build a killer LinkedIn profile" and just follow the steps.

Even if your background is not geared toward a professional office setting, recruiters and hiring managers may still look you up. If you make the effort to sign up, and have a nice profile, then it shows them that you are a savvy job seeker in the digital age. It's also a most necessary professional networking tool in today's age, especially for job seekers.

CHAPTER 4:

NETWORKING –
GETTING THE MOST OUT OF LINKEDIN

LinkedIn is the ultimate site for professional networking. Fortune magazine reported that as of April 2017, LinkedIn crossed the 500 million users mark with over 10 million job postings (http://fortune.com/2017/04/24/linkedin-users/).

I've been asked the question, "Should my LinkedIn profile mirror my resume?" The answer is "Absolutely Yes!" LinkedIn is not just a tool for showing your professional job history online and a place to apply for positions, but it is an incredible networking tool.

Networking is an incredible tool that can be used in many ways: to learn more about the latest trends in your profession or industry, to keep track of current and former employees, to enhance and promote your brand, to market products, to help others in their professional and job search needs, and of course, the most powerful tool, to help you find a new job!

The latter can be done in several ways. You can send a message out to all or selected people among your

First Connections to let them know you're looking for new employment.

This is exactly how I landed my last position. I sent out about 120 individual LinkedIn private messages to those in my LinkedIn network in the Kansas City area to let them know I was coming back to town and looking for a Recruiting Manager position.

I used a copy and paste method of the message content to hasten the process, but I did use each connection's first name in the greeting to personalize the message to them. Do not title a LinkedIn message, "Dear Connection". I have seen it before and it's not an effective or personal approach.

One of my LinkedIn connections, whom I also volunteered with in a local chapter of a professional organization, messaged me back to advise of a recruiting opening in her company, but it was only for a Recruiting Specialist position. She wrote, "Greg, I know this isn't the position you are looking for, but perhaps you can help us out with some recruiting while you're looking for a permanent role."

I thought, "Why not?" It's not a bad way to make some extra money while I continue my job search. I agreed to meet with her, and she got me in to interview with the president of the company. The interview went very well! I hit it off with the president and provided him with solid ideas and insights on how to improve their hiring processes.

About a week later, they changed the job title to Talent Manger, re-wrote the job description and gave me a very respectable offer for a position which I took. I otherwise would have never known about the position since I wasn't applying for Recruiting Specialist openings.

The total outcome of those 120 LinkedIn InMails resulted in 5 in-person interviews and 2 job offers!! These may not be typical results for everyone. The strength of my Kansas City network and the hot job market were contributing factors. But the fact is, hiring authorities want to hire someone they know about through people they trust.

This approach of leveraging your network can side-step the application process entirely and can lead to fast-tracking you to the interview stage, or even in the creation of a new, unpublished position suited to your strengths.

You never know who in your network has knowledge of an unpublished job, who could get your name and resume in front of a hiring manager, or who can get you to the top of the resume pile.

Another approach I am seeing more of these days is I see candidates putting their resume, accomplishments, and skills into a LinkedIn post and tagging their friends and LinkedIn Influencers to like and share the post. I've heard some job seekers finding success with this method.

There are a number of LinkedIn Influencers you should follow and connect with, especially if you are conducting a job search. They have anywhere from 10,000 to over 1.4 million followers each and they are passionate about helping job seekers as best they can. Keep in mind, most of them get dozens of requests daily for help, but it's still worth the effort.

Some of these key influencers are, **Oleg Vishnepolski, Brigette Hyacinth, Brett Brody, Adam Danyal, Ira Bowman, and Cory Warfield.** If you post your job search on LinkedIn, be sure to tag them. If you don't know how to tag someone on a LinkedIn post, just type the "@" symbol, then start typing their name, for example, @Oleg Vishnepolski. Then, select the correct name on the dropdown menu list that pops up. Now the person is tagged and he or she will receive a notification that they have been tagged in a post and can choose to like it or share it.

If you get lucky enough to have your post liked by Oleg Vishnepolski or Brigette Hyacinth, your post will get thousands of views.

<u>ADDED BONUS!</u> – I'll Post Your Resume!

If you send me a connection request, to Gregory Austin (type in https://www.linkedin.com/in/gregoryaustin1/ to your browser or search by my name on LinkedIn), and mention that you read my book, I will post your resume, skill set, and desired job on LinkedIn, tagging influencers. This can help you get exposure, connections, and hopefully an interview. Be sure to send me a personal note on the invite or through InMail, so I don't miss it. I receive a large volume of messages and connection requests, so please be persistent and I will follow up!

You can (and should) also use LinkedIn as a research tool to learn background on a hiring manager prior to an interview. This can help to give you talking points with the interviewer, especially if you both share a common interest. For example, if you both went to the same school, know the same people, or share a similar hobby.

You can also use the title or intro section of your LinkedIn profile as a banner to announce that you are seeking a new opportunity.

How to set up a great profile on LinkedIn.
First of all, make sure you set aside enough time to put together a solid profile, don't shortcut this

process! Like your resume, this is advertising your personal brand online, so make it the best you can.

This is a "professional" networking site, not Facebook, so make sure you are using a quality photo that is professional looking. Ask a friend or colleague with a good camera or camera phone to take the picture and dress up in a suit or other professional clothes that you would wear to an interview.

In some cases, depending on your profession or industry, it's okay to look more casual, which is fine, but don't use an unprofessional pose or show too much skin. Don't include spouses, kids, or unusual props.

Also, unless you are a photographer or fine artist, refrain from artsy or odd poses. Keep it simple and just smile directly at the camera. If you have a friend who is a photographer, then taking a picture in the city or your place of work with a blurred background is a particularly nice effect.

I recommend customizing your LinkedIn URL, don't settle for what they give you. You should customize it to your name. To accomplish this, click on the "Edit public profile & URL" button from your profile page, then click to "Edit URL" on the top right of the page and put in your name with no spaces. Someone else may already have that name/URL, so you may need to

add   a   number   to   it.   For   example,
"https://www.linkedin.com/in/<u>gregoryaustin1</u>/".

It is also a best practice to add this link to your email
signature to make it very easy for potential employers
to get a quick look at your background.

Write a headline that grabs attention! If you are
looking for a new job, then you shouldn't put your
current or most recent company and title. Instead,
you should write your "value proposition", what
makes you special, unique, and awesome.

For example, a marketing professional might use
"Direct marketing guaranteed to get you more
business." That would really stand out to anyone
looking for a direct marketing guru.

Use the Summary section to communicate who you
are, what makes you tick, and what your passions are.
You could pull from a prewritten cover letter if you
have one, but don't make it too formal. Keep it to
about 3-5 short paragraphs and write more casually,
like how you would speak to a colleague in a
professional setting. Use bullet points to highlight
important key facts.

Let your personality come through. Don't use much, if
any, jargon. It's much better to keep it authentic
rather than dazzling readers with technical terms.

Make sure you include keywords that help identify what you bring to the table so that recruiters can easily find you in a LinkedIn or Google search. Finally, proofread this section very, very carefully! Poor grammar and spelling errors will reflect poorly on you.

Your job history should absolutely mirror your resume. It creates legitimacy and consistency, especially when the hiring manager and recruiter inspect your LinkedIn profile. The last thing you want to do is to create confusion and doubt in the minds of an employer.

Be sure to include all your key accomplishments that are on your resume and be sure you are using those numbers that quantifiably demonstrate your performance and impact. Again, proofread and double check everything you put into it, for accuracy, spelling, and grammar.

Explore LinkedIn Groups by searching for areas that relate to your profession, industry, and interests. There are many professional groups out there, but you can also join sport fan groups and hobby groups that may provide another opportunity for networking.

From within those groups, you can post that you're looking for a job or something else of interest. The best backdoor feature is that you can also direct message other members of that group, even if you're not a First Connection with them. This can be a great method to communicate with potential employers or colleagues who can help you get better acquainted with them and perhaps get connected to others who can help.

Help with Changing Careers or Industries

I have worked with many candidates who wanted to change careers or transfer the same skill sets to a different industry. For some, the market for that industry was very saturated and there wasn't a strong presence of that industry in their city. For them, to continue in the same or an advanced role within their industry, they would most likely have to relocate.

For other candidates, they were simply ready for a new challenge, perhaps a bit bored with the same routine in the same job and industry.

Whatever the reason, it is a daunting task to make such a change without someone already offering a job in a new area from within your network. In most cases, candidates must consider taking a hit on their salary to get in at a lower level and prove their way up.

This perspective may make sense and may even work out as planned. In some rare cases, taking a brief cut in salary to prove yourself can get you promoted relatively quickly. However, this is usually not the case, so I urge caution when considering a pay cut.

Unfortunately, in our culture and society, most employers will consider the salary from your last job as the starting point for their offer. The general standard is to offer "up to" a 10% increase from the candidate's current salary. This offer amount is very relative to the average rate for that skill set, the needs of the company, the rarity of the candidate's skill set, and the number of qualified candidates available. Companies may offer a straight lateral in pay (i.e., the same amount), or they could offer a leap of 20% or more in salary, plus bonuses. Every situation is unique.

The moral of the story is if you take a pay cut in your next job, it will likely affect your ability to earn in the future, as the next company will probably base their offer on what you're making now, not what you earned in the past. I know this is true, because it happened to me. The consequence of this is it could take years just to get back to what you were earning just before you made a change.

Therefore, I urge you to consider this very carefully before accepting any kind of pay cut. The only caveat is if you were already earning well above the average for your position, education, and experience. Some companies simply pay better across the board (like Sprint), but when you start looking for a new position or get laid off, then you may find it difficult to obtain new employment because you are priced out of the market. Using sites like www.Salary.com or www.Payscale.com can help show you where your salary fits versus the average for that job title in your area.

The difficulty when changing careers or industries, is knowing where to go specifically and how to go about it. I have a good suggestion to help you in researching this yourself and the answer lies in using LinkedIn as a resource.

Let's say, for example, you have been a Site Director for a call center company for many years, but now you desire to take your operational knowledge and leadership experience to a new industry. Where would you go? The world looks like a mighty big place at this point.

What you can do is to find other call center Site Directors who have made a similar transition and track where they went, what their new title is, what industry they went to and look to see if they had to relocate in the process. Create a spreadsheet or a chart on paper and track all these data points.

Next, to find this data, you will want to search on LinkedIn for these people and research their profile to see what changes they made. You can search by title and industry (e.g., "call center site director"). This may generate a lot of results, relative to your own network (the larger your network of First Connections, the more results will be returned). This search will return mostly those who are currently in that role. You can use the "All Filters" button to give you more options to narrow the search and choose specific industries and titles.

Warning, this research will take time. Since you don't know what other Site Directors have changed to, then you can't be very specific in the search terms. You may consider adding the title you are interested in moving to, into the main search box or in the "Title" box of the All Filters section, as well as your current title. You will probably need to look through many pages of LinkedIn profiles and tweak your search in order to find what you're looking for.

Once you do find someone that has made a change which is congruent with what you want to do next, I urge you to connect with that person and explain in the connection request why you are connecting. Then, try to have a real-time conversation with that person over the phone, or even in-person if possible, to understand exactly how they made the transition. This will generate ideas on what new industries or job titles you can shoot for and strategize your job search around this.

If you already know exactly what you want to do next, but you're not clear how to get there, then I suggest you use the same strategy as above to find people on LinkedIn who are already doing that job, by searching on their job title. Once you find them, connect with them and see who will network with you to offer advice, and perhaps you may get lucky enough that they can connect you with the proper hiring manager who may consider you for the job. Keep in mind that not everyone is an open networker or able to help, but the more people you reach out to, the more likely you will find someone who is happy and eager to help.

Another approach, which should generate some results for you is to ask to find what you're looking for in a LinkedIn post. Be sure to tag many people (using the "@" symbol in front of their name and selecting them from the dropdown box). Tag friends, networkers, and influencers. The more people who see it, the better your chances of getting results. You may also receive some nice encouragement from the wonderful people on the LinkedIn platform.

CHAPTER 5 – COVER LETTERS

Cover letters do have a place in the job application process, and they can indeed help provide potential employers with insights to your passions, special abilities, accomplishments, and personality.

However, I am not a huge proponent of them. The reason is that even if the cover letter is brilliantly written and clearly shows how the candidate is an excellent fit for the role and the company culture, they actually don't get read much on the average.

The first reason cover letters do not get read often by most recruiters is because in most cases we are so pressed for time, that if the candidate is a strong fit, we will certainly discover that by reading the resume and quickly pass it along to the hiring manager. The cover letter at that point may be considered superfluous.

The second reason recruiters don't often read cover letters is because so many of them are either poorly written or do not add any value above and beyond the resume itself. Reading a very standard, basic cover letter in that case is typically a waste of time for busy recruiters. Certainly, a cover letter can help explain gaps in employment or demonstrate how personal passions and experience may overcome a lack of required experience, but even if the narrative is compelling, most hiring managers will opt to pass on that candidate in favor of resumes that are a better fit for the position.

DO NOT attach your cover letter to the first page of your resume. While this does draw direct attention to the cover letter, it confuses Applicant Tracking Systems and otherwise irritates the reader who wants only to evaluate a resume. The vast majority of employers will simply scroll down to the resume and may or may not go back to read the cover letter. If you are compelled to add your cover letter to your resume (which I do not recommend), then add it to the end of your resume.

Cover letters are not a bad thing per se and ironically, some employers still expect to see them, though this practice has dramatically reduced in contemporary recruiting.   With the speed of technology and business increasing rapidly, the reliance on the resume, LinkedIn profiles, and other social media outlets have become much more prevalent and the use of cover letters as an evaluation tool by employers has dropped.

Well written cover letters can only help, but even if your cover letter is brilliantly written, there is no guarantee it will get read. So, don't take it personally if your amazingly written cover letter does not lead to an interview.

ELEMENTS OF A GOOD COVER LETTER

To get started, a good cover letter should have the format of a standard business letter. If you have never written a cover letter before, you can search online for MS Word templates from within the MS Word application. Click on "File" then search for online templates by typing in "cover letter" and press enter.

Alternatively, you can simply conduct a Google search for cover letters and find free downloadable templates and examples for form, style, and content.

In the top left you should have your name and address with the date below it. If you know who the recruiter or hiring manager is, then you should address the letter to that person. It is unadvisable to write "To whom it may concern". That greeting is particularly cold and uninviting.

If you're not sure who may be reading your letter and the company is not unusually large, I suggest searching for the most probable hiring manager or recruiter on LinkedIn. The easiest way to do this is by first searching for the company in the search field in LinkedIn. Once you find their company page, you should see "People who work for..." on the top right.

Click on that link to view all their viewable employees who have a LinkedIn profile. From there you can filter by using keywords such as "recruiter", "recruiting", or "talent acquisition" to find the recruiter.

If you know what title should be interviewing for the position you are applying to, then search on that title and address the letter to the most appropriate person. Either is appropriate to use, even if use the hiring manager's name and the recruiter gets to it first.

If for any reason it's too difficult to determine the most appropriate person to address your cover letter to, it is acceptable to use "Dear Recruiter,".

The cover letter should begin with stating the position you are applying for and you should mention the company.

The next paragraph should get into what piqued your interest in the position and the company and why your skill sets are a particular fit for the position.

You should do some research on the company's Career Page online and get a feel for the company's mission, vision, and unique culture. Use that as material to explain how your background, personality, and career objectives are a good match. It will show the reader that you actually spent some time on their company's website, which shows much more interest and initiative than most other candidates applying for the same position.

This is a great opportunity for you to mention 1-2 chief accomplishments or top skills from your career. Make sure you match these achievements as closely as possible to the main needs mentioned in the job description.

Again, this takes more time and effort, but it will have a much greater impact than if you mention an accomplishment that has little to do with the direct needs detailed in the job description.

It's okay to mention personal volunteer contributions and achievements as space allows. Keep it as brief and easy to read as reasonably possible without deleting any key points and maintaining good structure and grammar.

Do not get too personal in the letter. If it seems necessary and relevant to address gaps in your resume, then you can mention that you took time off to take care of family or other personal matters, but you should most definitely avoid any gruesome details of your personal life, as previously mentioned. Keep that content brief, professional, and on point.

The only personal details you should mention should directly relate to why you are passionate about the company, position, or industry the company operates in.

Furthermore, do not get "cute" in your writing style or content. Avoid humor unless you are amazing at humorous writing and even then, be sure it's really necessary, helpful, and tasteful. In any case, completely avoid the use of sarcasm.

Be sure to sign the letter and you should scan a copy of it to make it easy to upload into the company's ATS online application or email directly to a potential employer.

Here is an example of a <u>very</u> poorly written cover letter:

(This letter was written at the top of a resume, not a separate document.)

John Doe
Adapt & Overcome
johndoe@indeedemail.com | 13335551212
Anytown, MO

I have 4 children

2 Boys in Sometown, Oklahoma

2 Girls in AnotherTown, Missouri

I am doing my best to be the Best Daddy I can possibly be.

Providing for my family is something I take very seriously and as such MY CAREER comes first as it ensures my children and myself Have a stable & secure environment for which to grow, learn, & develope our positive futures.

I am willing to try and pursue fields that may not be aligned with my training &/or experience as I am very confident in my ability to adapt and overcome in any environment or field of work as I will do whatever it takes to provide for my family.

To achieve this I intend on following through with the following statements each and everyday:

#1.) I will follow Direction of Leadership & work as a team as well as individually when necessary

#2.) I will Adapt & Overcome any and all possible situations that arise to ensure my personal work performance is more than within company requirements.

#3.) I will Follow all:

SAFETY Guidelines & Procedures

#4.) I will Attend and participate in any required or recommended training the company or leadership requests or requires of me

#5.) I will Show up 15min Early

#6.) I will Contact appropriate Supervisor if anything that may effect my work is to arise

#7.) I will be present for my shift

#8.) I will give 150%

#9.) I will take accountability for my actions and follow advised corrective measures when and if necessary

#10.) I will strive to be better each day than I was the day before through dedication and perseverance.

My goal is to be hard as possible to replace by preforming and working diligently in a manner for which it woukd take multiple people to replace me if possible.

Thank you for your time and consideration on this matter and I look forward to working with/for you if selected.

- -

There is a lot wrong this with this cover letter. What I did like about it, is that the letter conveys the candidate's desire to do the right things, to demonstrate good character, and show how and why he would be a good employee in general.

However, he starts out sharing way too much personal information. Sharing that he has kids in 2 different states may lead some people to think that he hasn't always made good decisions and may have an unstable personal life. Don't give potential hiring managers the chance to generate prejudging opinions about you before you even get your foot in the door for an interview. You could convey the same thing by simply writing "Providing for my family and having a stable career is very important to me. This is why I have chosen to apply to a stable and profitable company like ..."

Additionally, there are several spelling and grammar errors that could have been easily fixed by simply following the auto-spell checker (highlights misspelled words in red) and auto-grammar suggestions (highlights grammar issues in blue) provided by MS Word. Even Google Docs (which is free) has a spell checker function on it. Spelling errors should never occur on a cover letter and there are ways to get help with grammar by using Grammarly, which is also free, the grammar assistance in MS Word, or have a friend check it.

Finally, this is a very general cover letter. It does not address the specific position, how the candidate is qualified for that position, or how the candidate can add value to the needs of the position.

Also, do not connect the cover letter to the resume in the same document. It should be a separate document that stands on its own.

Here is an example of a very bland, general cover letter:

Dear Sir/Madam:

My name is XXXX, and I am responding to the posting for a new position in your organization. I am very interested in a job opportunity in your company.

In December 2017, I graduated with a Marketing Associate Degree at Johnson County Community College. Through the course I acquired a lot of practical experience in marketing. I attended many networking events with professionals and worked on the real project Tiny House 2018 at JCCC, which allowed me create and share marketing ideas with faculty.

During my school years at JCCC I worked mostly in Retail as a Sales Associate at Staples, Kohl's and JCCC Bookstore. My number one responsibility was working with customers, which helped me better understand their needs and wants, which is the base for the marketing sphere. I learned marketing techniques, which make stores successful, such as rebates, rewards programs and others.

More detailed information you will find in my attached resume. If you have any questions, please let me know. Thank you for your attention, and I am looking forward to meeting you in the future.

Sincerely,

XXXX

This is obviously a standardized cover letter this candidate created to send out to anyone for any kind of marketing position.

It's not personalized to anyone, nor is it customized to the job description. In this case, the position is for a Creative Marketing Intern position and doesn't reflect the needs of the position which include Photoshop and webinar experience.

In addition, there are a couple of grammatical mistakes that should have been avoided or corrected.

It's unlikely that any recruiters or hiring managers would read this. It's clearly a cut and paste job that is so non-specific that it could be directed to anyone for any related position.

It does not address a person specifically in the company, nor does it advise for what position the candidate has applied for, to say nothing about how the candidate may be qualified for the position or could otherwise add value to the company.

These are generally considered a waste of time for the candidate to create and send, as well as for the reader.

Here is an example of a very simple, yet strong cover letter:

Dear David:

I am writing in response to the opening for xxxx, which I believe may report to you.

I can offer you seven years of experience managing communications for top-tier xxxx firms, excellent project-management skills, and a great eye for detail, all of which should make me an ideal candidate for this opening.

I have attached my résumé for your review and would welcome the chance to speak with you sometime.

Best regards,

Xxxx Xxxx

Credit: https://hbr.org/2009/06/the-best-cover-letter Harvard Business Review

The above letter is very good for several reasons:

1. It's addressed to the apparent hiring manager.

2. It states the position applied for.

3. It's non-assuming. The phrases which exemplify this are "which I believe may report to you" and "would welcome the chance to speak with you sometime."

4. It's brief and easy to read.

5. It gets right to the point of how the candidate can benefit the company and why he or she is qualified for the position.

This is a very good example of a customized cover letter by a college student for a mechanical engineering internship:

Peter XXXX
XXX-XXX-XXXX | XXXX@XXXX.edu | XXXX N Main St. Olathe, KS 66061
December 12, 2017

XXXX XXXX
Director, Human Resources
XXXX, Inc.
XXXX Drive
XXXX, KS XXXXX

Dear Ms. XXXX:

Recently I was informed about the mechanical engineering internship by my mother, XXXX, regardless of her affiliation, I believe working for XXXX, Inc. would be a perfect fit from my personal research. Currently I am a sophomore at Kansas State University pursuing a Bachelors of Science in Mechanical Engineering. I was excited to read about modeling and drawing opportunities that would utilize my experience gained from drafting courses and share the want to make the world a better place with XXXX, Inc.

Over the past couple years my passion in the mechanical engineering industry grew and I am eager to apply myself to help in a professional engineering setting. While I was working at Mill Creek Pool as a head guard I learned about the pump systems for the pool and was responsible to help maintain the pool. I often received praise by my superiors due to the time and effort I put into making the pool better. The courses I have taken in college have made me familiar with all types of engineering. I specifically excelled in my graphics course where I earned a SolidWorks certification because 3D and 2D modeling sparked my interest because it gave me an opportunity to create and visualize my projects. I am passionate about learning more skills and applying myself towards a mechanical engineering career.

I am confident my skills, attitude, and passion will apply perfectly to the Mechanical Engineering Internship position at XXXX, Inc. I have what it takes to aid XXXX, Inc. in their goal to innovate and make the world a better place. If you have any questions regarding my application, feel free to reach out to me at XXXX or XXXX@XXXX.edu. Thank you for considering my application. I look forward to speaking with you.

Sincerely,

Peter XXXX

Enclosed: RESUME

There are several good things about this cover letter. First of all, the form itself is that of a formal letter and is properly formatted.

Secondly, he found a relevant employee in the company and addressed the letter personally to her. He also states the position applied to, so there is no confusion or ambiguity.

Next, he quickly gets to the point of matching his skills, passions, and qualifications to the needs of the position. He mentioned that he's in the appropriate bachelor program, Mechanical Engineering, and that he has some experience with 2D and 3D modeling with SolidWorks, a necessary requirement of the position.

He further impresses by stating his passions for mechanical engineering, the environment, and a knowledge of pumping systems (a main product manufactured by the company).

He concludes with positive language, "I am confident my skills, attitude, and passion will apply perfectly to the Mechanical Engineering Internship position" and reiterates his contact information.

This cover letter is on point, personalized, customized, and polite, but most importantly shows his ability to do the job.

Review of Cover Letter Tips

- Use a good, professional letter format.

- Personalize the letter to a specific recruiter or hiring manager.

- Be sure to mention the company name and position applied for.

- State why you are interested in the company and the position.

- State your qualifications based specifically on what's in the job description.

- Mention career achievements as it pertains to the job.

- Do NOT get personal, sarcastic, or use much humor.

- Restate your contact information and your interest.

- Don't assume anything, be too pushy or cheesy. (For example, "I just know you'll call me")

- Don't spend too much time on a cover letter. Use them when targeting special companies and positions that you really want.

- Remember, most cover letters will not get read, no matter how well they're written.

- Don't take it personally if they don't read your cover letter.

- Don't give up!

CONCLUSION

I hope you have found this book helpful and have been able to pull some gold nuggets out of it that you can use to tweak and fine tune your resume for greater effectiveness.

I also hope you found value in the chapter on networking. It is so key to adding speed, fun, and efficacy to your job search! Stay tuned for a future book dedicated to the Art of Networking.

I wrote this from my perspective, a Corporate Recruiter who reviews resumes all day for a living and as a former job seeker myself. It can be a difficult and arduous process and most people hate to do it. I sincerely want to help and make a difference for people who are just starting out or are in the middle of this tough, job-seeking process.

In summary, here are some of the key Have-to-Haves for your resume and job search:

1. Use a Chronological resume format.
2. Use a very clear format with consistent fonts and use bullet points.
3. Make sure your contact information is easy to find, and you use a simple, professional email address.

4. Get specific on your accomplishments, quantify them to numbers and communicate your value and impact to a company.
5. Put those accomplishments and key skills in your Professional Skills section and in your Job History.
6. **CUSTOMIZE** your resume, as best you can, to the job you are applying for, each time.
7. PROOFREAD, PROOFREAD, PROOFREAD!!! There should be NO mistakes on your resume, ever!
8. Build a killer LinkedIn profile.
9. Leverage the power of LinkedIn by networking daily, even when you're not in job search mode. This will always shorten and enrich the job search process.

If you found value in this book, please enter this web link into your browser:

https://www.amazon.com/dp/B07NTK6RG2

Scroll down to the Customer Reviews, then click on the "Write a customer review button".

Thank you and best wishes on your job search!

FREE BONUS!

For purchasing a copy of this book, I am offering a complimentary resume template, pre-formatted, in MS Word, to help get you started! Just fill it in with your own content!

To access this free template, enter this web link into your browser:

https://stellarresumewriting.com/freeresumetemplat e

Best wishes and good luck with your job and career search!

Made in the USA
Monee, IL
21 August 2022

12166938R00069